# The Moon: 60 Fascinating Facts For Kids

*Carl Johnson*

This book is just one of a series of "Fascinating Facts For Kids" books. For more fascinating facts about people, history, animals and much more please visit:

**www.fascinatingfactsforkids.com**

# Contents

# The Birth of the Moon

**1.** When the Solar System was formed around 4.6 billion years ago, it was a violent and unstable place. It wasn't unusual for planets and other heavenly bodies to collide with each other.

**2.** When the Earth was young - around 50 million years old - it was crashed into by another, slightly smaller planet. The incredible forces created by the collision sent enormous amounts of molten rock out into space.

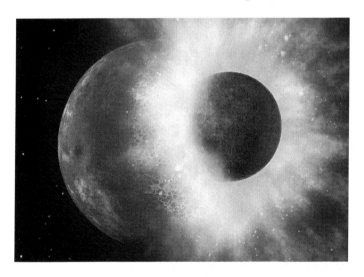

*The two planets colliding*

**3.** The debris from the collision went into orbit around the Earth, and gravity eventually gathered it all together to form the Moon.

**4.** The Moon today is a solid, rocky world around 240,000 miles (385,000 km) from the Earth. When the Moon was formed it was a hot, fiery place just 14,000 miles (22,500 km) away and would have looked massive and spectacular in the sky.

**5.** The early Moon was covered in volcanoes, and the lava which poured from them cooled to form vast, rocky plains on the surface. Around 800 million years ago, the volcanoes stopped erupting and the Moon cooled down to become the stark and barren world it is today.

*The Moon today*

# The Moon's Surface

**6.** The Moon's surface is covered in thousands of craters which were formed billions of years ago when the Solar System was young. Meteors and asteroids constantly crashed onto the Moon, blasting out vast amounts of rock and leaving behind hollow craters of all sizes.

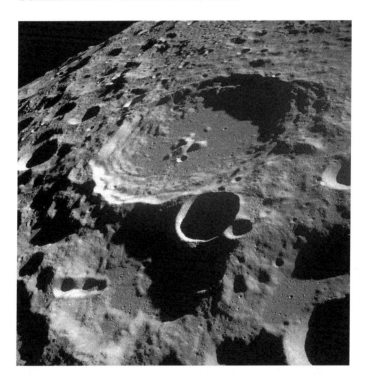

**7.** Because there is no wind or rain on the Moon to erode the landscape, the craters look much the same today as when they were first formed.

**8.** The largest crater on the Moon is called "South Pole-Aitken Basin." At 1,615 miles (2,600 km) wide and eight miles (13 km) deep, it is thought to be the largest crater in the Solar System.

**9.** Around 15% of the Moon's surface is covered in huge, dark plains known as the "seas." Early astronomers thought these areas were actually water-filled seas and oceans, but we now know that they are made of ancient, solidified lava.

Seas

**10.** The seas of the Moon were given romantic, Latin names such as "Mare Tranquillitatis" (Sea of Tranquility) and "Mare Nubium" (Sea of Clouds).

**11.** Huge mountain ranges surround many of the Moon's seas. These "Lunar Highlands" appear brighter than the darker seas, as they are made up of a different and much older type of rock.

Mountains

**12.** The constant bombardment by countless meteors and asteroids eventually ground the surface of the Moon into dust and rubble. This "lunar regolith" can be as deep as sixteen feet (5 m) and covers virtually the whole of the Moon.

# The Moon's Orbit

**13.**   The Moon is constantly moving round the Earth, taking just over twenty-seven days to complete each orbit. The Moon also spins once on its axis every orbit, which means that the same side of the Moon is always facing the Earth and we never see the far side.

**14.**   The path of the Moon's orbit round the Earth is in the shape of an ellipse rather than a perfect circle. This means that the distance between the Earth and the Moon varies during the course of an orbit and the closer the Moon gets to the Earth, the larger it appears in the sky.

**15.**   The closest the Moon gets to the Earth is around 221,500 miles (356,500 km) and the furthest distance is around 252,700 miles (406,700 km).

**16.**   When the Moon reaches its closest point to the Earth - known as the "perigee" - it can appear 10% bigger in the sky than when it is at its furthest point - the "apogee."

# The Lunar Cycle

**17.** The Moon does not emit any light of its own. It appears so bright because light from the Sun is reflected off its surface. The half of the Moon facing the Sun is lit up and the other half, facing away from the Sun, is in darkness.

**18.** As the Moon orbits the Earth it appears to change shape from one night to the next. This is because we see the Moon from different angles as it travels round the Earth, and so the amount of the bright surface we see changes every night. These changes in shape are called "phases" - each one having a different name.

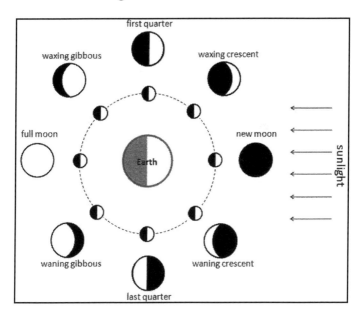

*The phases of the Moon*

**19.** The first phase is called the "New Moon," where the Moon is positioned between the Earth and the Sun. The illuminated half of the Moon faces away from the Earth and the side facing us is in darkness. We only see the Moon faintly by the small amount of light reflected onto it from the Earth.

**20.** A week after the New Moon, the Moon has completed a quarter of its orbit, and half of its near side is visible from the Earth. This phase is called the "First Quarter."

*The First Quarter*

**21.** When the Moon is halfway through its orbit the whole of the side facing the Earth is lit up, and the whole circle of the Moon is visible. This phase is called the "Full Moon."

*The Full Moon*

**22.** A week after the Full Moon, the Moon reaches the "Last Quarter," and the Sun shines on the opposite side to the First Quarter, again showing half the Moon visible from the Earth. After another week, the Moon completes its journey when it reaches the starting position of the New Moon.

**23.**　There are also phases between the First and Last Quarters and the New Moon called "Crescents," where we see the Moon in the shape of a narrow crescent.

*A Crescent Moon*

**24.**　The phase between the New Moon and the First Quarter is called the "Waxing Crescent." "Waxing" means "growing," and the Moon appears to be getting bigger in the early part of its journey round the Earth.

**25.**　The phase between the Last Quarter and the New Moon is called the "Waning Crescent." "Waning" means "growing smaller," and the Moon appears to be shrinking as it comes to the end of its journey round the Earth.

**26.** The phases between the Full Moon and First and Last Quarters are called the "Waxing Gibbous" and the "Waning Gibbous". "Gibbous" comes from the Latin word for "hump," and the amount of the Moon we can see is shaped like a hump, with more than half the surface visible.

*A Waxing Gibbous Moon*

# Eclipses

**27.** During the New Moon phase, the Moon doesn't usually pass *exactly* between the Earth and the Sun, but on the rare occasions that it does a "solar eclipse" occurs, when part of the Earth is plunged into darkness during the day.

**28.** A solar eclipse happens when the Moon moves directly in front of the Sun, gradually stopping its light from reaching the Earth. The Moon isn't big enough to cast its shadow over the whole of the Earth, so solar eclipses are only visible from a small area of the planet.

*A solar eclipse*

**29.** The Sun is 400 times bigger than the Moon, but also 400 times further away, which is why the Sun and the Moon appear to be the same size in the sky.

**30.** "Total eclipses" - where the Moon covers the Sun completely - occur somewhere on Earth about every eighteen months. A slightly more common type of eclipse is the "partial eclipse," when the Sun and Moon do not line up exactly and the Moon only partially covers the Sun. During a partial eclipse it looks as though the Moon has taken a bite out of the Sun.

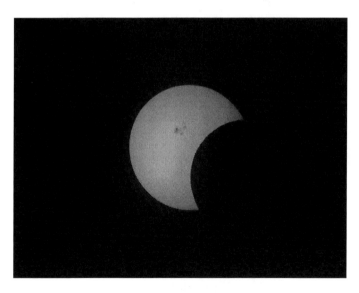

*A partial solar eclipse*

**31.** Another type of eclipse is the "lunar eclipse," which occurs during the Full Moon phase when the Earth is positioned between the Sun and the Moon. The Earth's shadow is cast onto the surface of the Moon, turning it an orange-red color for a couple of hours.

**32.** While it is safe to watch a lunar eclipse with the naked eye, it is very dangerous to look directly at a solar eclipse or the Sun itself without special eye protection.

# Tides

**33.** The Earth's gravity holds the Moon in orbit, but the weaker gravity of the Moon has an effect on our planet, causing the tides of the oceans and seas.

**34.** The Moon's gravity pulls the land areas of the Earth towards it by around an inch (2.5 cm), but the waters of the oceans are stretched by up to ten feet (3 m).

**35.** High tides occur on the side of the Earth facing the Moon, but the centrifugal forces of the planet's rotation means that there will be a high tide on the opposite side of the Earth at the same time. In between these areas the low tides appear.

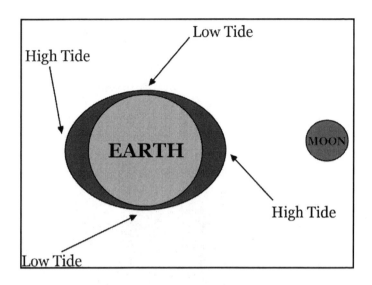

*The Moon and the tides*

**36.** The combination of the Earth's rotation and the Moon's gravity sweeps the tides around the world every day, producing daily high and low tides along the coasts of all the Earth's oceans.

**37.** The Sun's gravity also affects the tides, although its pull is much less than that of the Moon. When the Sun and the Moon are in alignment during the New Moon and Full Moon phases, their combined gravity produce the highest high tides and the lowest low tides, known as "spring tides."

**38.** During the First and Last Quarters of the Moon's orbit, the Sun and the Moon are at right angles to each other and their combined effect is much weaker. During these times the least extreme tides occur, lower high tides and higher low tides, which are called "neap tides."

**39.** In the distant past, when the Moon was much closer to the Earth, the Moon's gravitational pull was much stronger and the tides much more extreme. It is thought that these early tides helped to create the conditions for life to begin on Earth.

# Myths & Legends

**40.**  Throughout history, mankind has been fascinated by the Moon. Many ancient civilizations worshipped the Moon as a god, and countless myths and legends have been created about the Earth's nearest neighbor.

**41.**  4,000 years ago, the people of Mesopotamia (present-day Iraq) built a massive temple, or "ziggurat," in the city of Ur. Here they worshipped their Moon god, Nanna. A small shrine was placed on top of the ziggurat to be the place on Earth where Nanna could live.

*The Ziggurat of Ur*

**42.**  The ancient Egyptians believed the Crescent Moon to be the horns of a mighty bull that had died and been placed in the sky. The bull comes back to life and grows stronger as the Moon appears to become bigger during its orbit. By the time of the Full Moon, the bull is at its most powerful.

**43.** Around 5,000 years ago, in southern England, Stone Age people constructed a massive stone circle called Stonehenge. The true purpose of Stonehenge is a great mystery, but the stones may have been placed to line up with the Sun and Moon and to predict solar eclipses.

*Stonehenge*

**44.** In medieval Europe, it was thought that the Full Moon could transform human beings into wolves, the most feared wild animal on the continent. These fierce "werewolves" had superhuman strength and speed, and have been the subject of countless books, movies, and TV shows.

**45.** On the eighth Full Moon of every year, when the Moon is at its brightest, the Chinese celebrate their "Moon Festival." This ancient festival is a day of thanksgiving following a good harvest. The traditional food eaten at the Moon Festival is the "Mooncake," which is a rich, sweet pastry often filled with a cooked egg yolk to represent the Moon.

*Chinese mooncakes*

# Man on the Moon

**46.** Men have gazed up at the Moon for centuries dreaming of one day traveling to it. By the middle of the twentieth century the technology had been developed to attempt the dangerous and difficult journey.

**47.** In the years following World War Two, which ended in 1945, there was a great rivalry between the United States and the Soviet Union. Both countries wanted the prestige and honor of being the first to send a man to the Moon.

**48.** In the early days of what was known as the "Space Race," the Soviets were way ahead of the Americans. On April 12, 1961, a Soviet cosmonaut called Yuri Gagarin became the first man to be launched into space, completing one orbit of the Earth before landing safely back in Russia.

**49.** The US responded by sending astronaut Alan Shepard on a fifteen-minute flight into space, and on February 20, 1962, John Glenn became the first American to orbit the Earth.

### *John Glenn*

**50.** The Soviet space missions became more and more ambitious and successful, and the US president, John F. Kennedy, was worried that the Soviets would beat America to the Moon. He gave billions of dollars to the US space program and pledged that American astronauts would land on the Moon before the end of the decade.

*President Kennedy delivers his pledge to Congress*

**51.** The US space agency began the "Apollo" program, sending a series of unmanned rockets into orbit round the Earth where they tested equipment and techniques to prepare for a flight to the Moon. The first manned Apollo mission, Apollo 7, was launched in October 1968, successfully orbiting the Earth with three astronauts on board.

**52.** On December 21, 1968, Apollo 8 was launched, and five days later it was in orbit round the Moon. The three astronauts on board were the first human beings ever to see the far side of the Moon. Although Apollo 8 didn't land on the Moon, the success of the mission meant that the US was getting ever closer to fulfilling President Kennedy's pledge.

***"Earthrise" seen from Apollo 8***

**53.** On July 16, 1969, Apollo 11 blasted off from Cape Canaveral in Florida and five days later, Neil Armstrong and Buzz Aldrin left the Moon's orbit to land their lunar module on the surface of the Moon. When Armstrong descended the steps of the spacecraft to become the first human being to put his feet on the Moon, he spoke the now famous words, "That's one small step for a man, one giant leap for mankind."

***Buzz Aldrin on the Moon***

**54.** Hundreds of millions of people from all over the world watched the Moon landing on TV. Armstrong, Aldrin, and the third Apollo astronaut, Michael Collins, returned to Earth as heroes and were given a traditional ticker-tape parade through the streets of New York City.

**55.** Other Apollo missions followed Apollo 11, each one bringing back more information about the Moon. In all, twelve men walked on the Moon, the last one being in 1972, and it is hoped that it won't be too many years before man sets foot on the Moon's surface once again.

# Assorted Moon Facts

**56.** When the Sun is completely hidden by the Moon during a total eclipse, solar prominences are often visible. These are enormous solar flares of burning gas which leap from the surface of the Sun, often forming huge, fiery arches.

**57.** When the Italian explorer, Christopher Columbus, was stranded on the Caribbean island of Jamaica in 1504, he knew that a New Moon was due. When it happened he told the frightened Jamaican natives that the Moon would only return to normal if they helped him. The trick worked, as the islanders helped Columbus and his crew leave the island to be rescued later.

*Christopher Columbus*

**58.** The moon gets very hot during the lunar day and very cold at night. The temperature can get as high as 273°F (134°C) during the day and as low as -245°F (-154°C) on the Moon's dark side.

**59.** The gravity on the Moon is much less than on the Earth and there is no atmosphere. These two factors enabled Apollo 14 astronaut Alan Shepard to hit a golf ball for half a mile (0.8 km) over the Moon's surface.

**60.** The Moon is moving away from the Earth by around one and a half inches (3.8 cm) every year. This means that in hundreds of millions of years from now the Moon will be too far away to cover the Sun completely and so there will be no more total eclipses.

# Illustration Attributions

**The two planets colliding**
NASA/JPL-Caltech [Public domain]

**Craters (Fact 6)**
NASA (photo by Apollo 11) [Public domain]

**Seas / Mountains (Facts 9 & 11)**
Peter Freiman [CC BY-SA 3.0
(https://creativecommons.org/licenses/by-sa/3.0)]

**The phases of the Moon**
Andonee
https://creativecommons.org/licenses/by-sa/4.0/deed.en
https://creativecommons.org/licenses/by-sa/4.0/legalcode

**The First Quarter**
NASA Goddard Space Flight Center from Greenbelt, MD, USA [CC BY 2.0
(https://creativecommons.org/licenses/by/2.0)]

**A Crescent Moon**
David Moug [CC BY 3.0
(https://creativecommons.org/licenses/by/3.0)]

**A Waxing Gibbous Moon**
Kevin [CC BY 2.0
(https://creativecommons.org/licenses/by/2.0)]
http://www.flickr.com/photos/kevincollins/110708833/

Made in the USA
Las Vegas, NV
02 December 2023